Thinking Theory
BOOK TWO
Written by Nicola Cantan

www.colourfulkeys.ie

© 2016 Colourful Keys. All Rights Reserved.

WARNING! The contents of this publication are protected by copyright law.
To copy or reproduce them by any method is an infringement of the copyright law.

What is Thinking Theory?

→ Thinking Theory is a series of music theory workbooks designed to accelerate learning while providing plenty of reinforcement of each concept.

→ No topic is introduced without being revisited several times later in the book.

→ The flashcard games provide a unique way to learn away from the page, and make learning and teaching more secure and more fun.

→ The "Level Up!" tests at the end of each chapter and book allow you to evaluate student learning and plan their next step.

Concepts covered in this book...

→ Note values: sixteenth note, eighth note, dotted eighth note, quarter note, dotted quarter note, half note, dotted half note & whole note

→ Rest values: sixteenth rest, eighth rest, quarter rest, half rest & whole rest

→ Time signatures: $\frac{2}{4}$ $\frac{3}{4}$ $\frac{4}{4}$

→ Landmark notes: low C, bass C, bass F, middle C, treble G, treble C & high C

→ Note stem rules

→ Grouping sixteenth notes, eighth notes & rests in simple time

→ Dynamics: pianissimo, piano, mezzo piano, mezzo forte, forte, fortissimo, crescendo & diminuendo

→ Tempo marks: ritardando, rallentando, allegro, allegretto, moderato, andante

→ Expression marks: dolce, grazioso & cantabile

→ Markings/symbols: accidentals, staccato, slurs, repeat marks, fermata, accent, tenuto, 1st and 2nd endings, 8va & 8vb

→ Solfa: do, re, mi, fa, so, la & ti

→ Scales: C major, G major, D major & F major

→ Triads: C major, G major, F major & F major

→ Whole steps, half steps & enharmonics

Contents

New concept pages are shown in bold.

Chapter 1	**Note Values** 1		Chapter 4	**Note Stem Rules** 22	
	Note Stem Rules 2			**Rhythms** 23	
	Landmark Notes 3			**Solfa Singing** 24	
	Scales: C Major & G Major 4			**Scales: F Major** 25	
	Solfa: Do, Re, Mi & So 5			Solfa Writing & Singing 26	
	Dynamics 6			**Terms & Symbols** 27	
	Level Up! Chapter 1 Test 7			Level Up! Chapter 4 Test 28	
Chapter 2	**Note Naming** 8		Chapter 5	**Grouping Sixteenth & Eighth notes** 29	
	Note Drawing 9			Scales 30	
	Note & Rest Values 10			**Grouping Rests** 31	
	Solfa: La 11			Terms & Symbols 32	
	Solfa Writing & Singing 12			Solfa Writing & Singing 33	
	Tempo Marks 13			**Major Triads** 34	
	Level Up! Chapter 2 Test 14			Level Up! Chapter 5 Test 35	
Chapter 3	**Time Signatures: 2:4, 3:4 & 4:4** 15		Chapter 6	Level Up! The Final Test 36	
	Accidentals 16			Level Up! The Final Test 37	
	Scales: D Major 17			Level Up! The Final Test 38	
	Solfa: Fa & Ti 18				
	Terms 19				
	Terms & Symbols 20				
	Level Up! Chapter 3 Test 21				

About Nicola Cantan

Nicola Cantan began teaching piano in 2004, and has always strived to find new ways to engage students in learning. She uses games, improvisation and composing to accelerate her students' progress at the piano and broaden their musical knowledge.

Nicola wrote the 'Thinking Theory' books when she saw the struggle some of her students were having preparing for theory examinations. She wanted a book that regularly reinforced concepts in a systematic way, with a clean layout and clear explanations. Thus 'Thinking Theory' was born.

FLASHCARD GAMES

All the flashcard games can be played with the corresponding Thinking Theory Flashcards which can be downloaded at www.colourfulkeys.ie/thinking-theory.

To play these games, the cards will need to printed one-sided, with the answer on a separate card. You may want to print two sets, one to be used as regular flashcards (printed back to back) and one to be used for games (printed on one side).

You can play these games with the flashcards for one or more chapters at a time, or with the complete set for the whole book. Games like this are a fantastic way to reinforce learning off the page, and allow drilling of concepts in a fun way. Try to revisit each flashcard set periodically by playing a different game, to foster long term and reliable memory.

MEMORY

1. This is a game for one or more players.
2. Lay out all the cards face down.
3. Turn over two cards at a time. If they match, put those cards aside. If they don't match, turn them back over.
4. Keep going until all cards have been matched.

(This game can also be played with multiple players taking turns.)

MATCH

1. This is a game for one player.
2. Layout all the term cards face-up on the floor.
3. See how fast you can match the answer cards, by placing each card on top of the term that matches.
4. Time yourself and try to beat your time on the next go!

PAIRS

1. This is a game for two or more players.
2. Shuffle the cards and deal 4 to each player. Place the remainder of the cards in a pile between the players..
3. Each player takes turns to draw one card from the pile in the centre.
4. If s/he has a matching pair, s/he should place it face up beside them.
5. The winner is the one with the most pairs when all the cards have been drawn.

© Copyright 2016 Colourful Keys

SNAP

1. This is a game for two players.
2. Shuffle the cards and divide into two equal piles, one for each player.
3. On the count of three both players turn over the top card from her/his pile.
4. If the cards match, either player can shout "SNAP!".
5. The first player to say "SNAP!" wins all of the turned over cards, and adds them to her/his pile.
6. The winner is the first to win all the other cards, or the one with the most cards when time is up.

GO FISH!

1. This is a game for two or more players.
2. Shuffle the cards and deal 5 to each player. Place the remainder of the cards in a pile between the players..
3. Each player takes turns to ask another player for cards that would match one of her/his own. For example "Got any E's?" or "Got a crescendo?".
4. The player can continue asking for more cards until the other player does not have the card they need, and tells them to "Go fish!".
5. If told to "Go fish!" the player should pick up a card from the centre pile.
6. As pairs are found, they should be placed face down in front of them.
7. The winner is the first to get rid of all her/his cards. If two players do this at the same time, the winner is the one with the most pairs.

CUCKOO

1. This is a game for two or more players.
2. Remove one card from the deck and place it aside.
3. Shuffle the cards and deal all the cards between the players. It's OK if some players may get more cards than others.
4. Each player should sort through the cards and put down any pairs s/he finds, without letting the other players see her/his cards.
5. One player at a time offers her/his cards (face down) to the player to her/his left.
6. The player to the left takes one card from her/his hand.
7. If this makes a pair, the player to the left puts the pair down beside her/him.
8. Continue like this until all the pairs have been found. The player left with the "Cuckoo" is the loser.

Chapter 1

Thinking Theory Book Two

New Ingredients: Note Values

♪ = eighth note = ½ beat
♩ = quarter note = 1 beat
𝅗𝅥 = half note = 2 beats
𝅗𝅥. = dotted half note = 3 beats
𝅝 = whole note = 4 beats

𝄽 = quarter rest = 1 beat
▬ = half rest = 2 beats
▬ = whole rest = whole measure

✏️ Practice drawing the new ingredients.

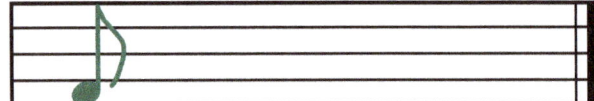
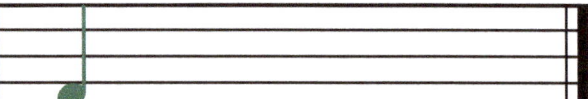
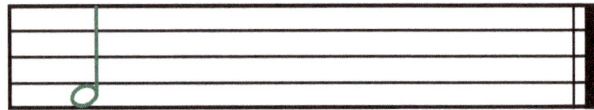
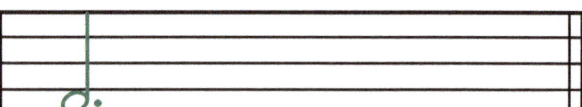
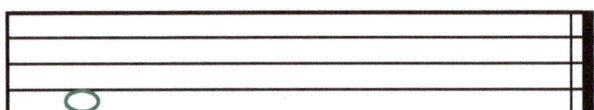
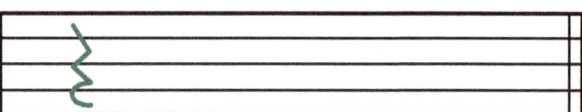
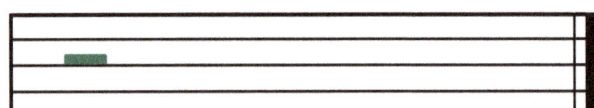
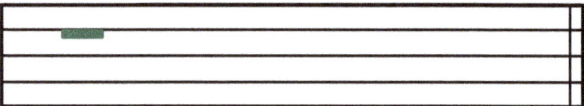

✏️ Connect rectangles and circles with matching numbers of beats.

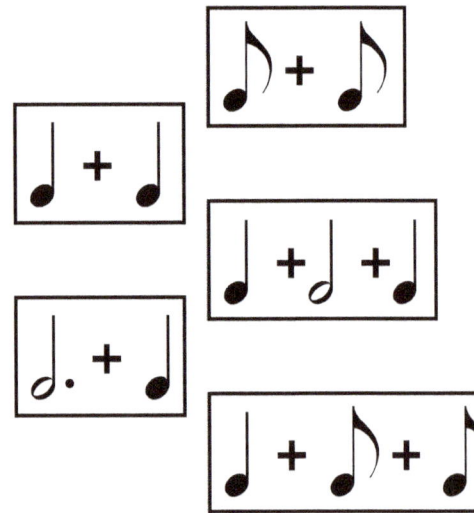
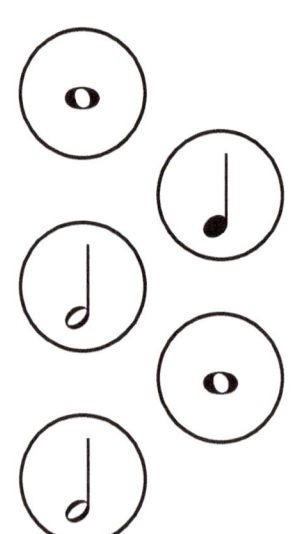

© Copyright 2016 Colourful Keys

→ Note Stem Rule 1: If the note is line 3 or above, the stem goes *down* on the *left* of the notehead. If the note is space 2 or below, the stem goes *up* on the *right* of the notehead.
→ Note Stem Rule 2: The stem should finish at the same note an octave above for upward stems, and at the same note an octave below for downward stems.

 Copy each note below and notice how they follow the stem rules.

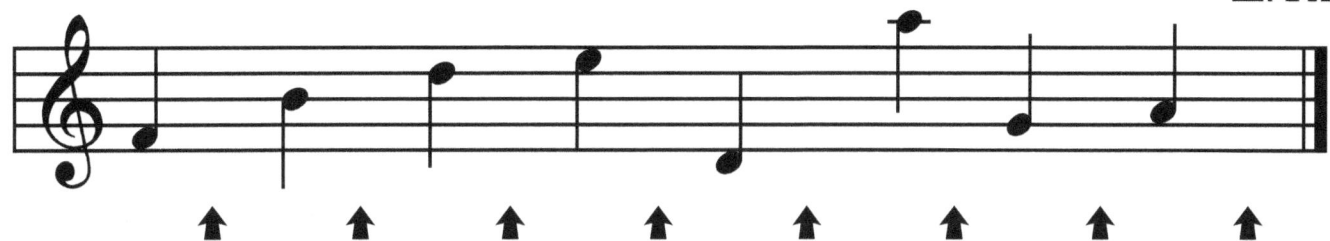

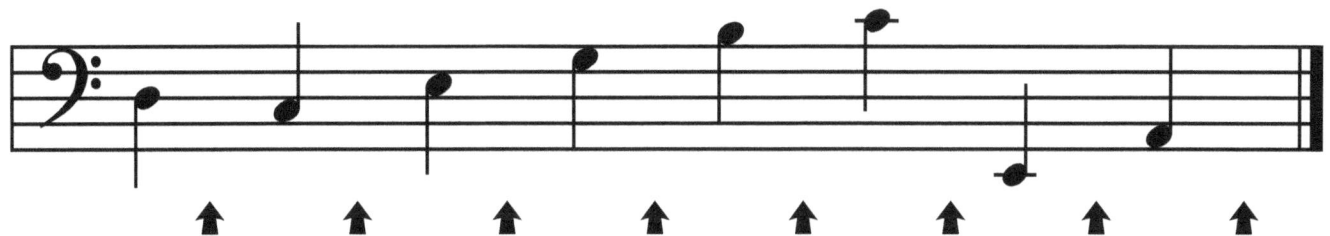

 Complete each quarter note by drawing the note stems.

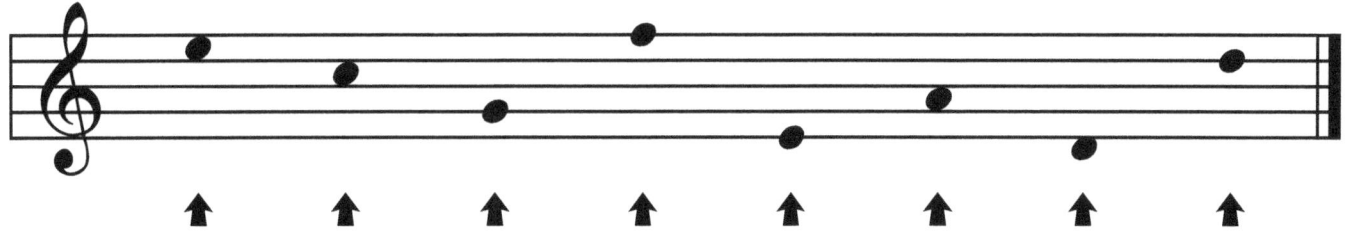

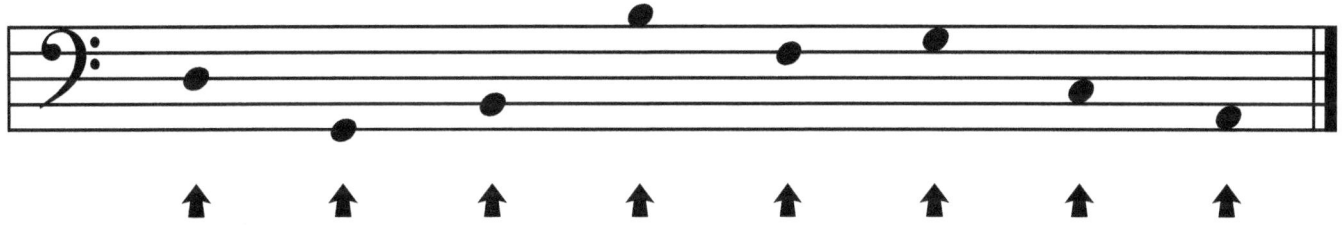

Chapter 1

Thinking Theory Book Two

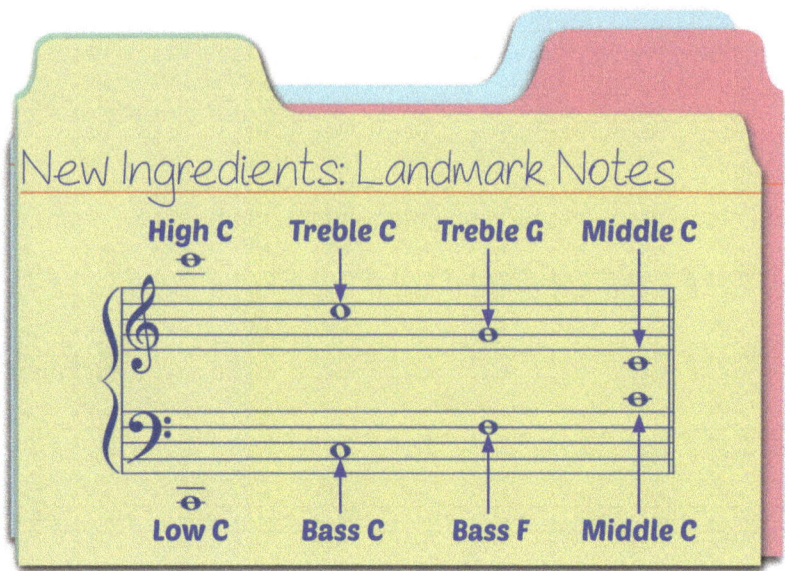

→ These 8 notes are often known as "landmark notes". If you know your landmark notes well, you can figure out any other note by working your way up or down the staff.

→ High C and Low C do not follow 'Note Stem Rule 2' from the previous page. Their stems will finish at the middle line.

 Draw...

10 Middle C quarter notes.

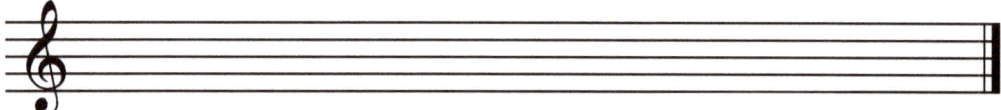

8 Treble C whole notes.

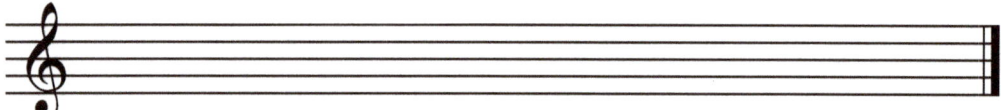

12 Bass F quarter notes.

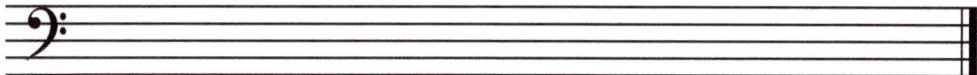

10 High C half notes.

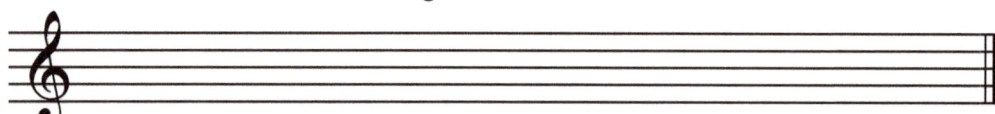

8 Low C half notes.

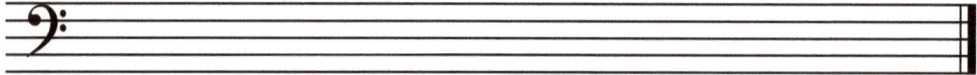

6 Bass C dotted half notes.

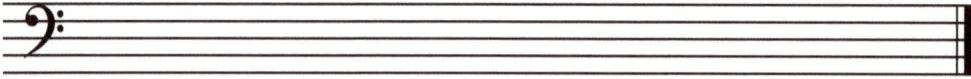

Chapter 1

New Ingredients: Scales

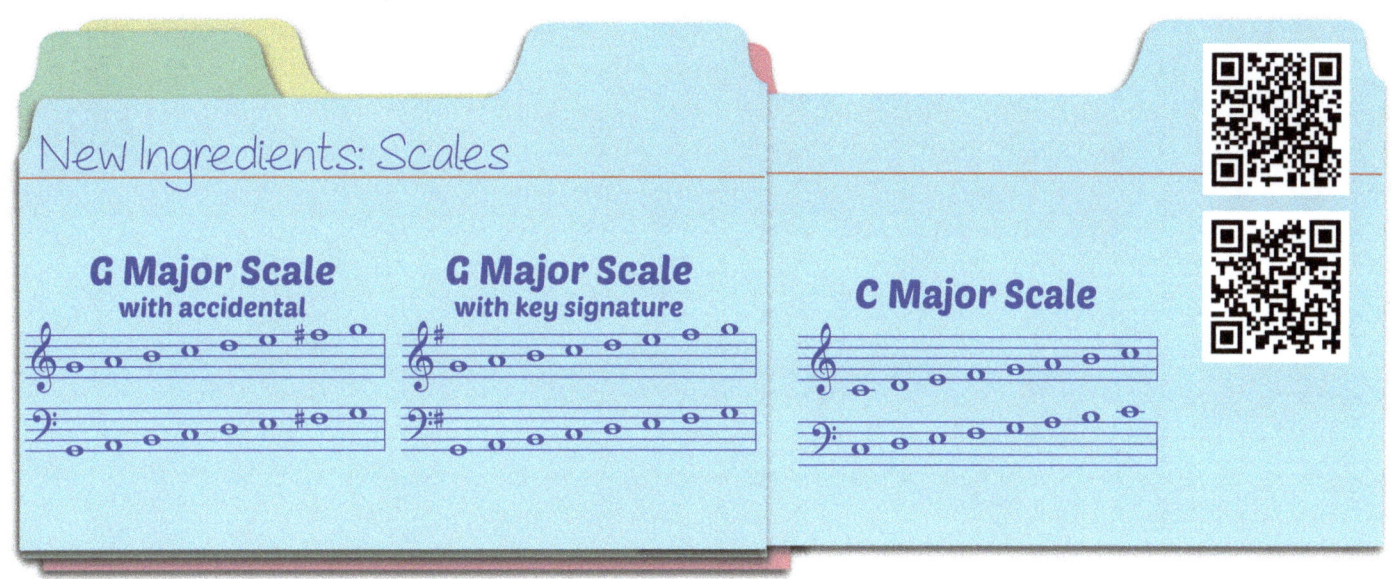

✏️ Color in the keys used in the C major scale.

✏️ Color in the keys used in the G major scale.

✏️ Write the...

C major scale, descending, in quarter notes.

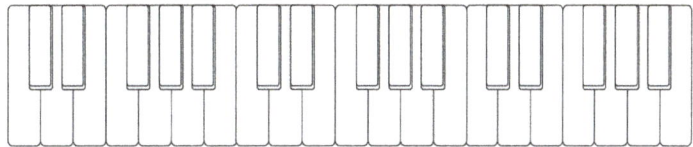

G major scale, ascending, in whole notes with accidentals.

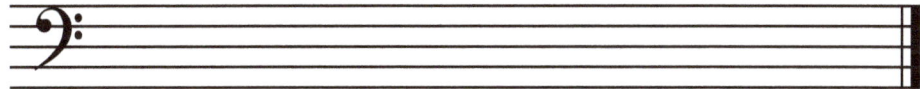

G major scale, descending, in half notes with key signature.

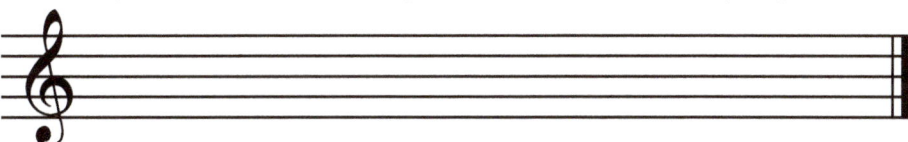

Chapter 1

Thinking Theory Book Two

🎵 Practice singing the exercises below, using the solfa hand signs.

d r d r d r d r d r d r d r d r d r d r d r d r

d r m r d r m r d r m r d r m r d r m r d r m r

d r m r d r d r d r m r d r d r d r d r

d r m s m r d r m s m r d r d r m s

d r m r m r m s m s m s m r d r m r d d

d r d r m s s m r d d r d r m r m m s s

d r m s s m m r d d r r d r m m s m s m

✏️ Write the musical symbols in the boxes, from loudest to softest.

☐ ➤ ☐ ➤ ☐ ➤ ☐ ➤ ☐ ➤ ☐

✏️ Fill in the blanks with the Italian terms. Then read the complete story aloud.

The antelope creeped past the sleeping lion, as __(very soft)__ as he could. The lion's snores were __(soft)__ and for a moment all was well. But then the antelope stepped on a twig, which made a __(moderately loud)__ snap. The snap awoke the sleeping lion who roared __(very loud)__!

✏️ Mark the statements as true or false.

Mezzo forte is louder than forte.	True ☐ False ☐
Piano means play loudly.	True ☐ False ☐
Pianissimo is softer than piano.	True ☐ False ☐
Fortissimo is softer than forte.	True ☐ False ☐
Mezzo forte means moderately loud.	True ☐ False ☐
Forte is softer than fortissimo.	True ☐ False ☐
Pianissimo means moderately soft.	True ☐ False ☐

Chapter 1   Thinking Theory Book Two

Level Up!
Get ready for chapter 2 by answering these questions (without looking back through your book!)

1. Write in the note names under each of these notes.

_____   _____   _____   _____   _____

2. Draw notes on the staff for each of these notes.

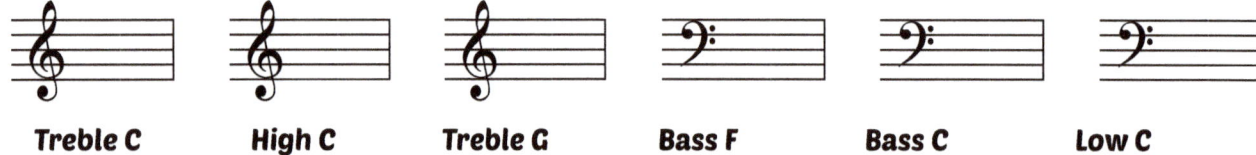

   Treble C   **High C**   **Treble G**   **Bass F**   **Bass C**   **Low C**

3. Write the time name and number of beats for each of these notes and rests..

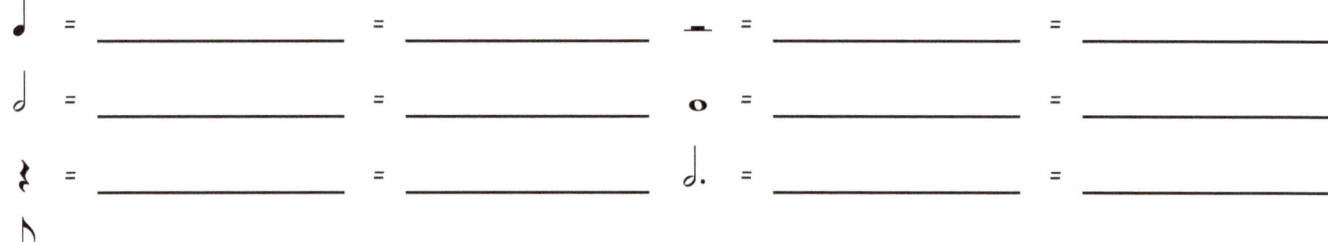

4. Label each solfa hand sign.

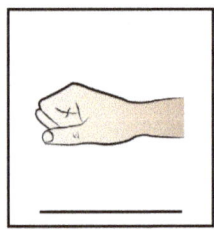   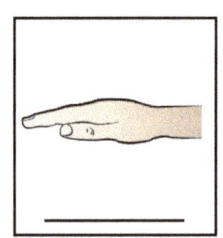   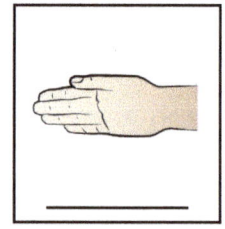   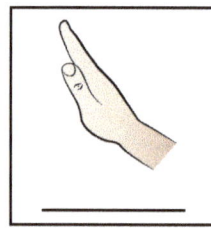

_____   _____   _____   _____

5. Fill in the full italian terms and meanings for each musical symbol below.

   mf = _____ = _____   *f* = _____ = _____

   pp = _____ = _____   *p* = _____ = _____

   mp = _____ = _____   *ff* = _____ = _____

6. Write out the G major scale, ascending and descending, with the key signature, in half notes.

Thinking Theory Book Two — Chapter 2

→ We can use the landmark notes learned in the previous chapter to work out any other note. Simply work your way up or down the staff from the closest landmark note.

✏ Identify each note below. The landmark notes are shown in grey as a guide.

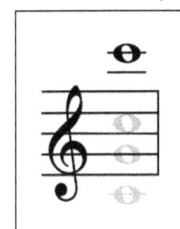     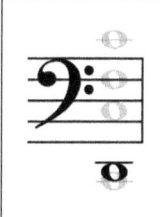

___ ___ ___ ___ ___ ___

    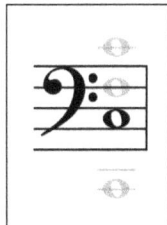 

___ ___ ___ ___ ___ ___

___ ___ ___ ___ ___ ___

     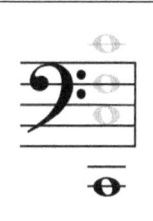

___ ___ ___ ___ ___ ___

___ ___ ___ ___ ___ ___

Chapter 2

➡ Review the stem rules from Chapter 1 before completing this exercise. Remember that 'Low C' and 'High C' stems finish at the middle line.

➡ To make it clear which note is being asked for, notes will be referred to as low, bass, treble or high. For the purpose of this exercise, this is defined as follows:

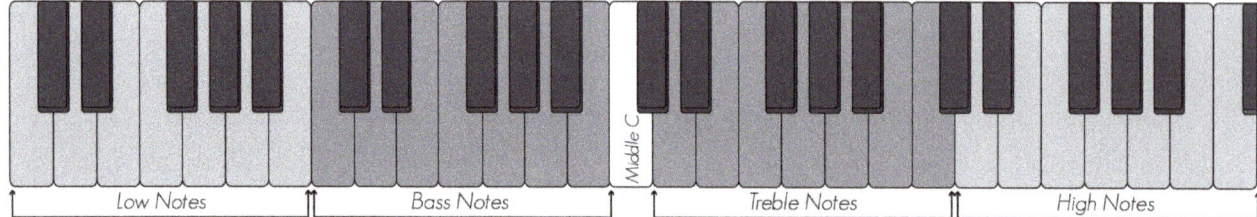

✏ Draw each of these notes on the staff, as quarter notes.

High G	Treble C	Treble E	Low G	Bass D	High F	Bass F	Low C

Treble F	High E	Low E	Bass C	Low A	Treble A	High D	Bass B

Low B	Low D	High B	Bass G	Bass A	Treble G	High A	Treble B

New Ingredients: Note Values

𝄿 = sixteenth rest = ¼ beat

𝄾 = eighth rest = ½ beat

♪. = dotted eighth note = ¾ beat

𝅘𝅥𝅯 = sixteenth note = ¼ beat

✏️ Practice drawing the new ingredients.

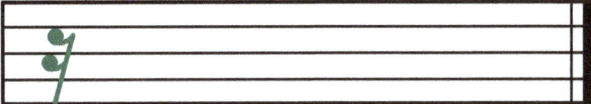 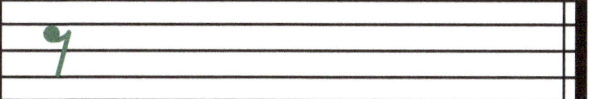

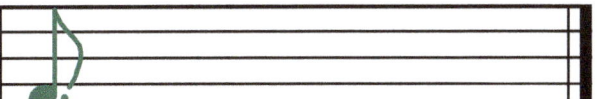 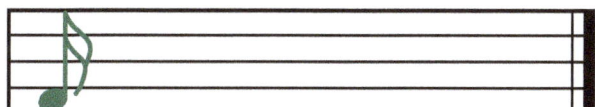

✏️ Draw lines to connect the matching numbers of beats.

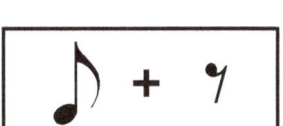

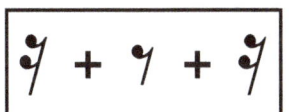

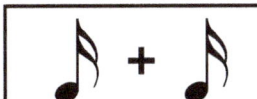

Chapter 2 — Thinking Theory Book Two

New Ingredients: Solfa

la

> → In the last chapter, you learned the solfa names 'do', 're', 'mi' and 'so.'
> → 'la' comes after 'so' in the solfa scale.
> → These five notes are also known as the "pentatonic scale".

🎤 Practice singing the exercises below; first with, then without, the aid of a piano.

✏️ Label each note with its solfa initial.

🎤 Practice singing the exercises below; first with, then without, the aid of a piano.

> Solfa melodies can be written as simple rhythm notation (sometimes called 'stick notation') with solfa names or as staff notation.

✏️ Rewrite these solfa notations on the staff, using the scale of C major.

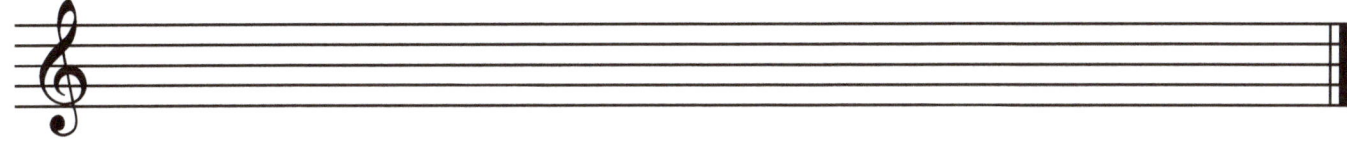

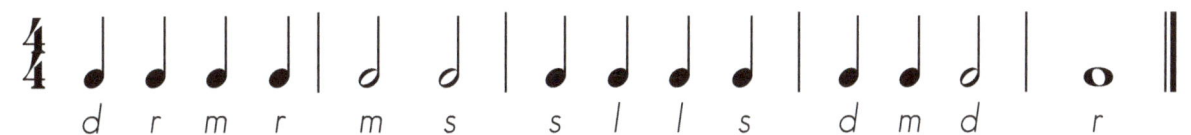

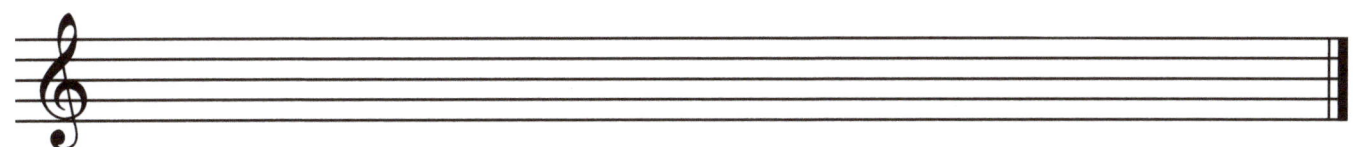

✏️ Rewrite these solfa notations on the staff, using the scale of G major.

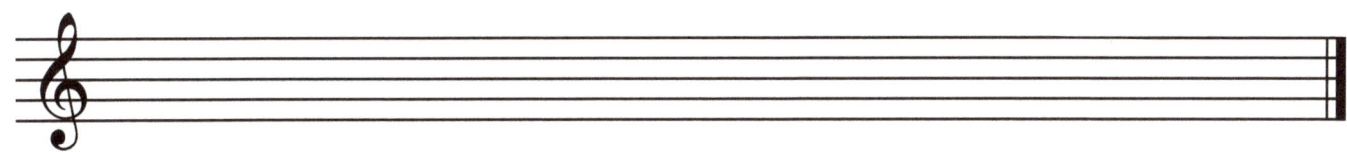

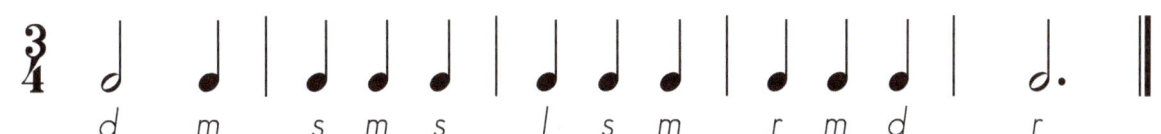

New ingredients: Tempo Markings

- *allegro* = quick & lively
- *allegretto* = moderately quick & lively
- *moderato* = moderate speed
- *andante* = walking pace
- *largo* = slowly
- *adagio* = slowly

New ingredients: Changes of Tempo

- *rit.* = gradually getting slower
- *ritard.* = gradually getting slower
- *rall.* = gradually getting slower
- *poco rall.* = gradually getting a little slower
- *poco rit.* = gradually getting a little slower
- *accelerando* = gradually getting faster
- *a tempo* = back to original speed

 Circle the correct answer to each question.

Which of these is the fastest?	*allegro*	*andante*	*largo*	*allegretto*
Which of these is the slowest?	*moderato*	*allegretto*	*andante*	*allegro*
Which of these means to play a little slower?	*adagio*	*allegretto*	*poco rit.*	*ritard.*
Which of these means back to original tempo?	*largo*	*moderato*	*a tempo*	*accelerando*
Which of these means walking pace?	*adagio*	*andante*	*moderato*	*largo*
Which of these tells the performer to slow down?	*adagio*	*rall.*	*largo*	*andante*

 Put an 'X' through the boxes that are incorrect.

- *poco rit.* = *poco rall.*
- *ritard.* = *rit.*
- *poco rall.* = *ritard.*
- *rit.* = *rall.*
- *rit.* = *a tempo*
- *rall.* = *poco rall.*
- *accelerando* = *a tempo*
- *poco rit.* = *a tempo*
- *a tempo* = *poco rit.*
- *poco rall.* = *poco rit.*
- *accelerando* = *rall.*

Thinking Theory Book Two — Chapter 2

Level Up!
Get ready for chapter 3 by answering these questions (without looking back through your book!)

1. Write in the note names under each of these notes.

____   ____   ____   ____   ____   ____

2. Draw half notes on the staff for each of these notes.

Treble D   **High F**   **Treble A**   **Bass A**   **Bass E**   **Low B**

3. Write the time name and number of beats for each of these notes and rests..

♩ = _____   = _____   𝄾 = _____   = _____

𝄾 = _____   = _____   ♪ = _____   = _____

𝄽 = _____   = _____   𝅗𝅥. = _____   = _____

♪. = _____   = _____   — = _____   = _____

4. Label each solfa hand sign.

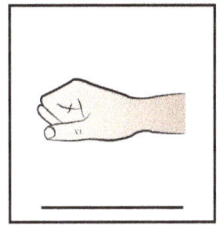 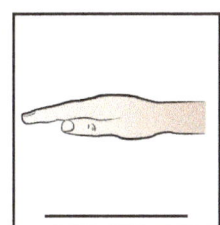 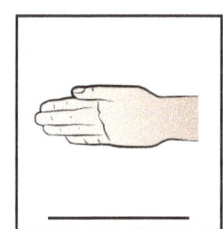 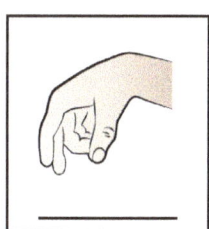 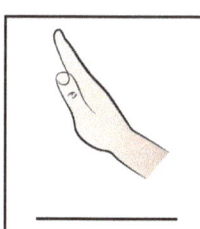

5. Fill in the meanings for each musical term below.

allegro = _____   *andante* = _____

accelerando = _____   *poco rall.* = _____

rall. = _____   *allegretto* = _____

largo = _____   *moderato* = _____

rit. = _____   *a tempo* = _____

adagio = _____   *poco rit.* = _____

Chapter 3 — New Ingredients: Time Signatures

- $\frac{2}{4}$ = 2 quarter note beats in a measure (simple duple time)
- $\frac{3}{4}$ = 3 quarter note beats in a measure (simple triple time)
- $\frac{4}{4}$ = 4 quarter note beats in a measure (simple quadruple time)
- $\mathbf{C}$ = 4 quarter note beats in a measure (simple duple time)

✏️ Fill in the missing time signatures.
👏 Practice clapping the rhythms.

✏️ Fill in the missing barlines.
👏 Practice clapping the rhythms.

✏️ Create your own 4 measure rhythms in $\frac{2}{4}$, $\frac{3}{4}$ & $\frac{4}{4}$.
👏 Practice clapping the rhythms.

- A half step is the distance between *any* two adjacent notes.
- On a keyboard this could be a black key and a white key, *or two white keys.*
- 'Enharmonic notes' are notes which are written differently but sound the same, e.g. 'G sharp' and 'A flat'.

New ingredients: Terms & Symbols

half step = interval between two adjacent notes
whole step = two half steps
enharmonic = two notes which sound the same
♯ = sharp = one half step lower
♭ = flat = one half step lower
♮ = natural = not sharp or flat

Mark the whole steps and half steps in the G major scale with a 'W' or 'H'.

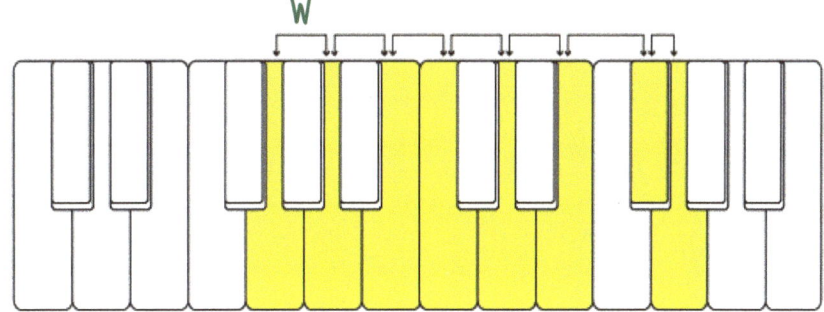

Color these notes on the keyboards
If the note has an enharmonic, draw it on the second staff.

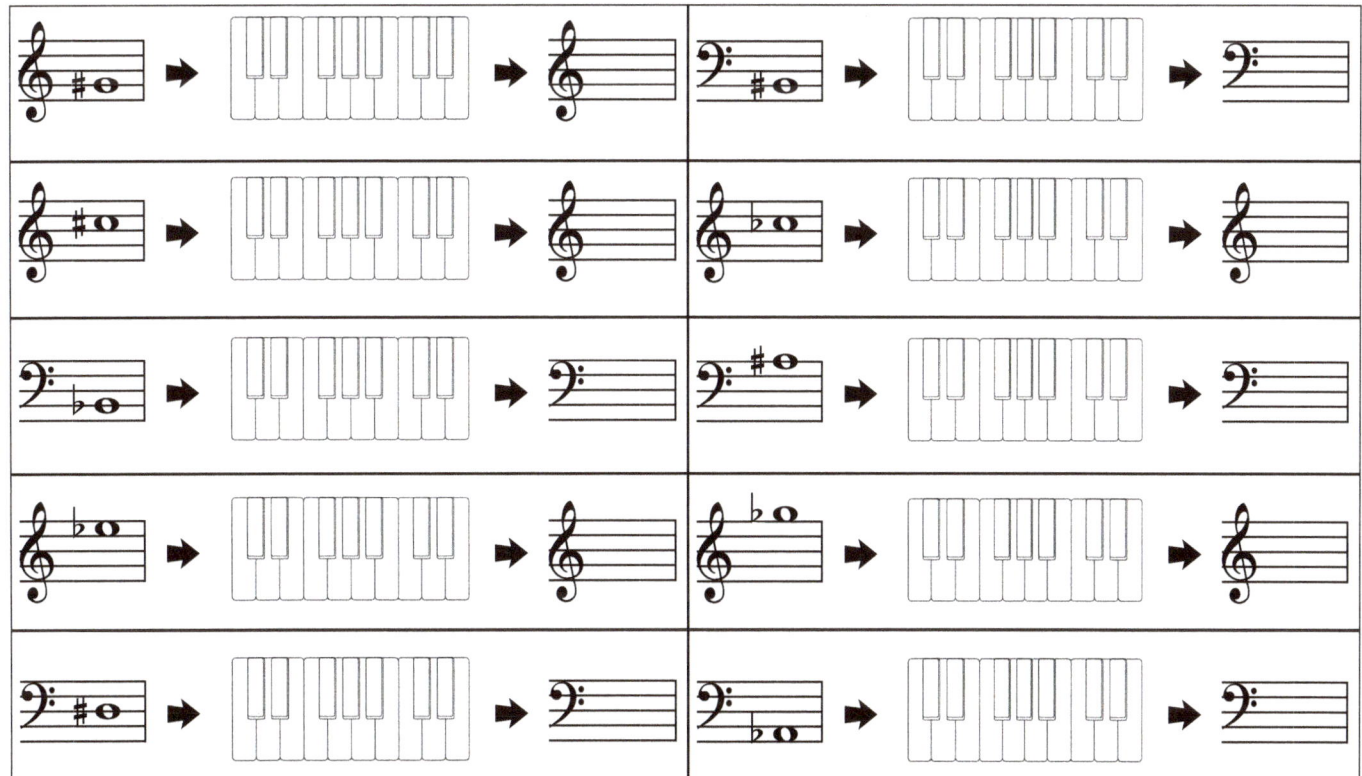

Chapter 3 Thinking Theory Book Two

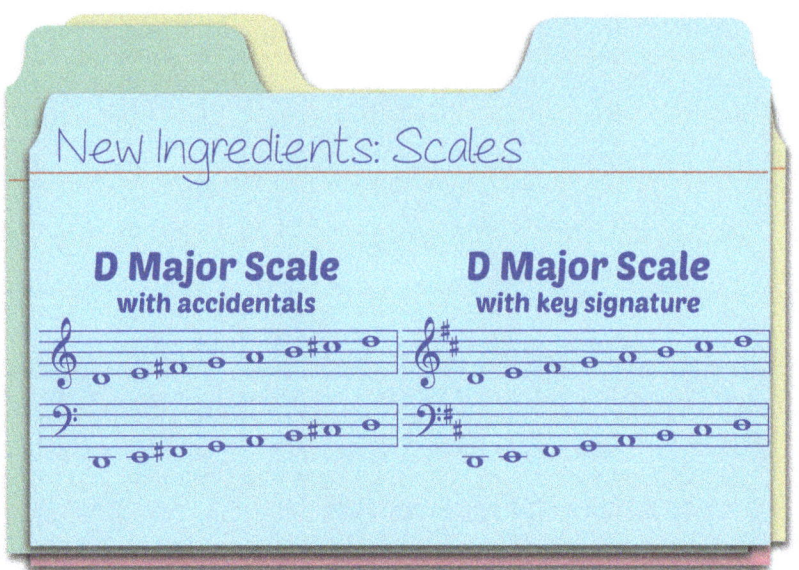
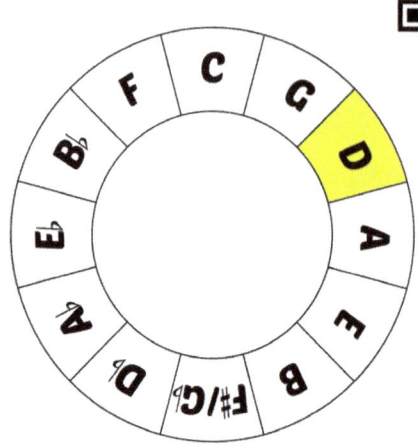

✏️ Color in the keys used in the D major scale. Mark the whole steps and half steps.

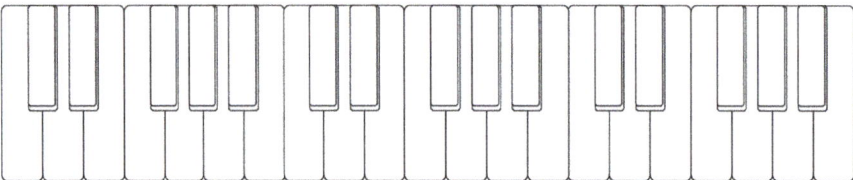

✏️ Rewrite this solfa notation on the staff in the key of D major. Use accidentals.

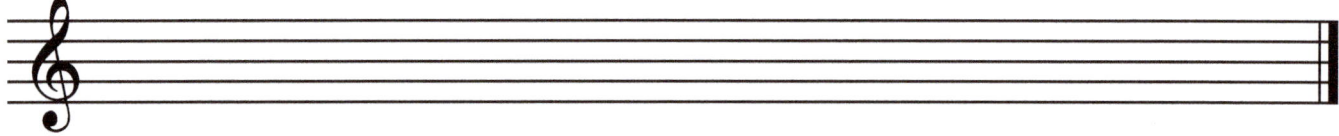

✏️ Rewrite this solfa notation on the staff in the key of D major. Use a key signature.

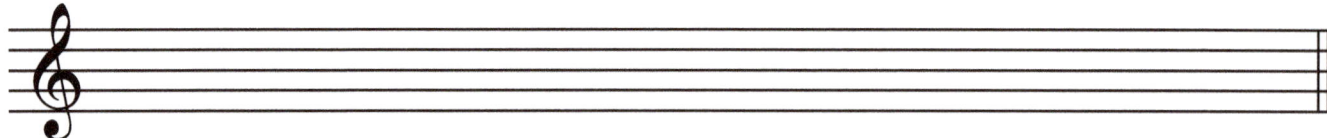

Page 17 © Copyright 2016 Colourful Keys

So far we have been using a pentatonic scale for solfa. To sing a complete major scale we need two more notes.

The note 'fa' comes after 'mi' and before 'so'.

The note 'ti' comes after 'la'.

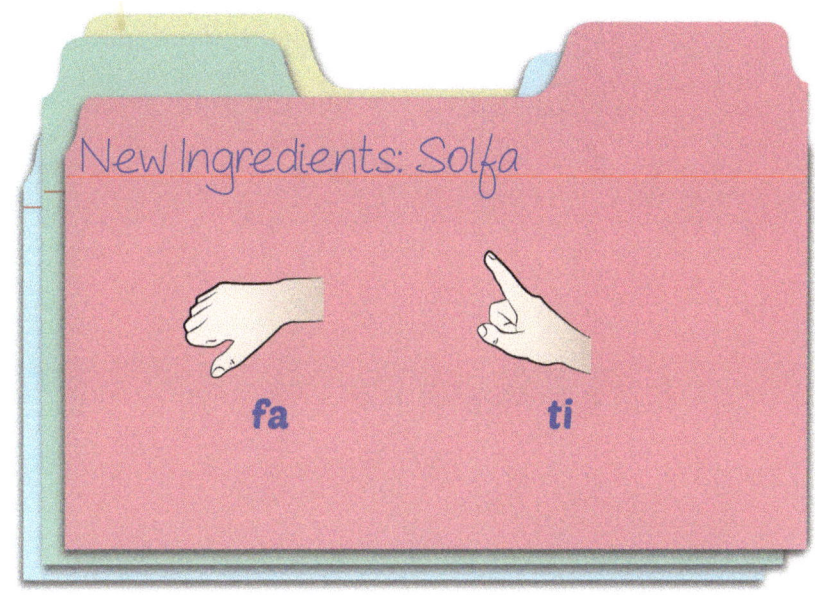

Practice singing the exercises below; first with, then without, the aid of a piano.

Label each note with its solfa initial.

Practice singing the exercises below; first with, then without, the aid of a piano.

✏️ Match the musical symbols/terms to their meaning.

pp	very loud
mf	getting a little slower
allegro	slowly
rit.	getting faster
accelerando	very soft
largo	moderately soft
poco rall.	moderately quick & lively
mp	getting slower
andante	getting slower
a tempo	soft
allegretto	getting a little slower
ff	moderately loud
ritard.	quick & lively
f	getting slower
moderato	back to original speed
adagio	moderate speed
rall.	loud
poco rit.	walking pace
p	slowly

Thinking Theory Book Two — Chapter 3

✏️ Label each picture with the new musical term that best suits it.

_____   _____   _____

✏️ Add markings to the score below to show that:

1. Measure 2 & 5 should be played staccato in the treble clef.
2. The piece should start with a two note slur in the treble clef.
3. Measures 4-8 should be repeated.
4. The piece should be played with a singing tone.

Level Up!

Get ready for chapter 4 by answering these questions (without looking back through your book!)

1. Write the tempo marks in the boxes, from fastest to slowest: **allegro**, **moderato**, **largo**, **andante**, **allegretto**.

   ☐ → ☐ → ☐ → ☐ → ☐

2. Draw a note one half step higher beside each of the notes below.

3. Draw a note one whole step lower beside each of the notes below.

4. Write the scale of D major, descending, in the bass clef. Use a key signature.

   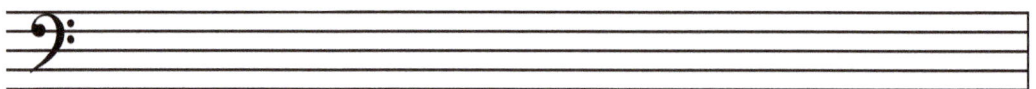

5. Draw one note value in each space to complete the measures.

   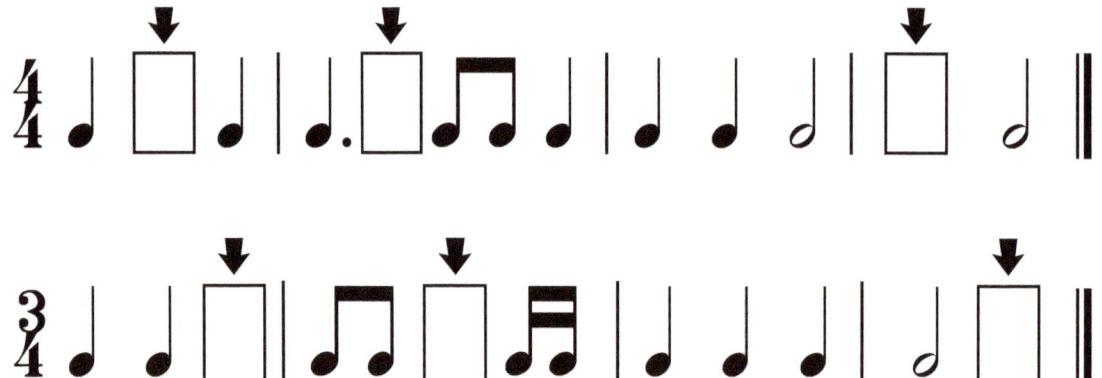

6. Fill in the meanings for each of these terms.

   rallentando = _____   grazioso = _____

   cantabile = _____   adagio = _____

   accelerando = _____   moderato = _____

   dolce = _____   diminuendo = _____

Thinking Theory Book Two — Chapter 4

 Label each of the notes below.
 Put an 'X' through any notes which are drawn incorrectly.

Finish each of the rhythms below using a variety of note values, and write the counts under the rhythms.

Practice clapping the rhythms.

 | | | ‖

 | | | ‖

 | | | ‖

 | | | ‖

Thinking Theory Book Two — Chapter 4

✏️ Label each note with its solfa initial (the first one is done for you).

🎵 Practice singing the exercises below; first with, then without, the aid of a piano.

d m m f m s l t t l s l s m r m

Chapter 4   Thinking Theory Book Two

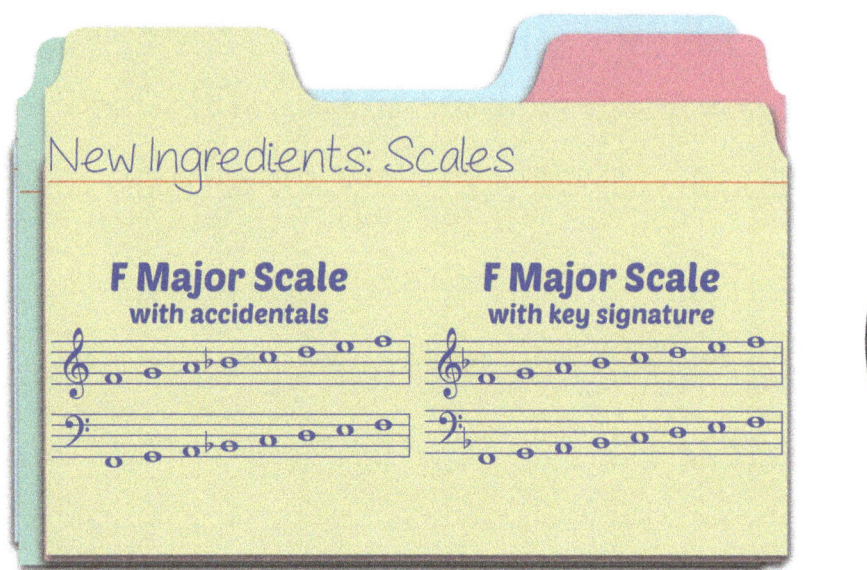
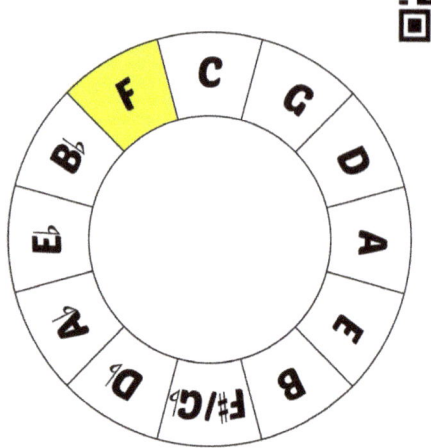

✏️ Color in the keys used in the F major scale. Mark the whole steps & half steps.

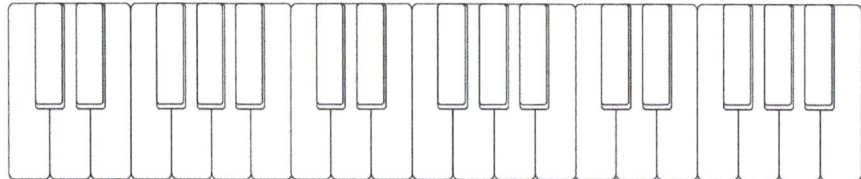

✏️ Rewrite this solfa notation on the staff in the key of F major. Use accidentals.

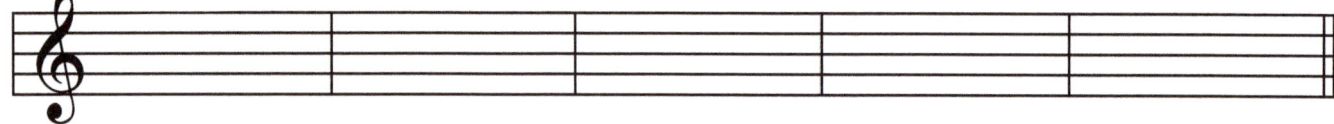

✏️ Rewrite this solfa notation on the staff, in the key of F major. Use a key signature.

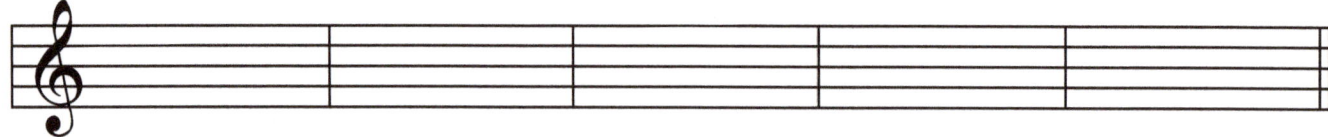

Rewrite this solfa notation in each of the keys below.

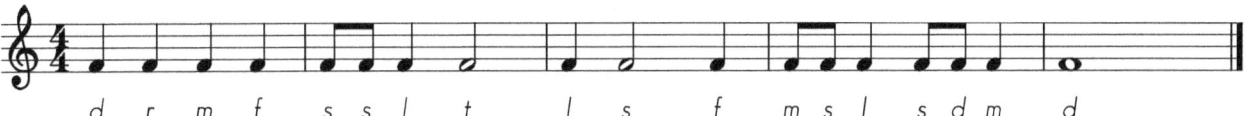

C Major

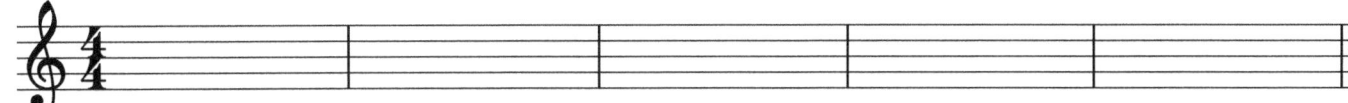

G Major

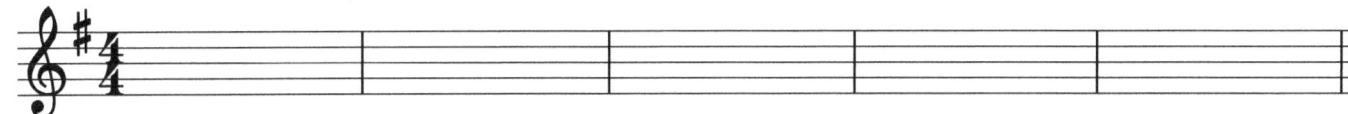

D Major

F Major

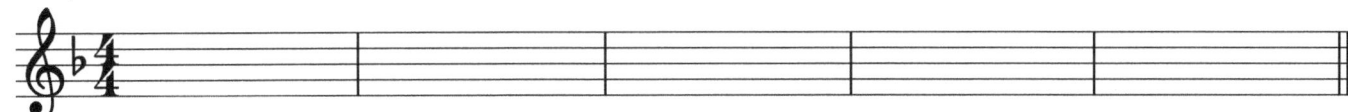

 Rewrite this solfa notation in each of the keys below.

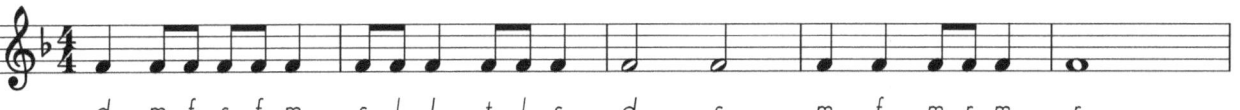

C Major

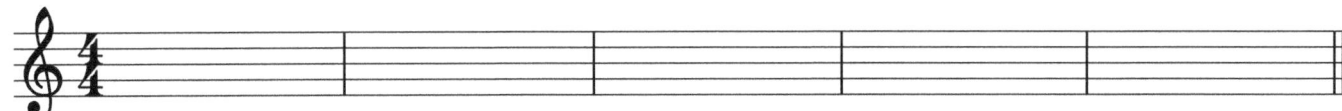

G Major

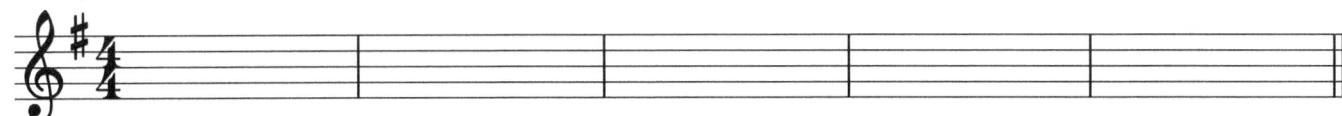

D Major

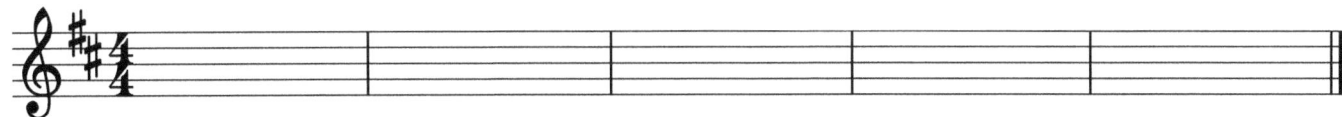

F Major

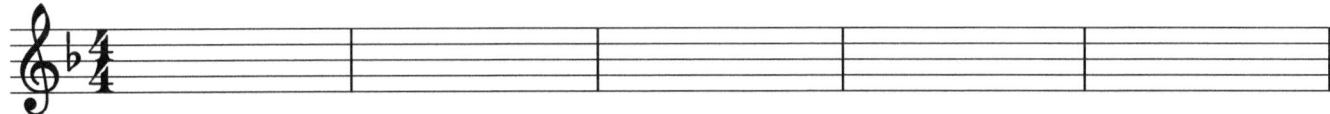

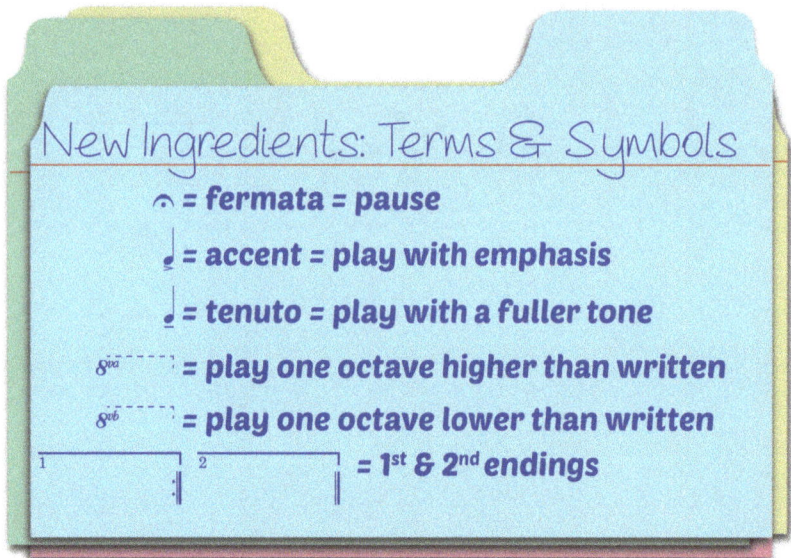

 Add markings to the score below to show that:

1. When the first phrase in the treble clef is repeated, it should be played one octave higher.
2. The player should pause on the final note of each line.
3. The piece should start quietly, and get louder in the second half.
4. The first note of each phrase should be played with emphasis.
5. The second line should be played twice.
6. The piece should be played quickly.

 Answer these questions about the piece.

1. What is the note name of the highest note in the piece? _____

2. Is the time signature duple, triple or quadruple? _____

3. Which major key is the piece in? _____

Level Up!

Get ready for chapter 5 by answering these questions (without looking back through your book!)

1. Draw an enharmonic beside each of the notes below.

2. Draw quarter notes on the staff for each of these notes.

      G sharp   **A**   **E sharp**   **G**   **B flat**   **C**

3. Write the scale of F major, ascending. Mark the half steps and use accidentals.

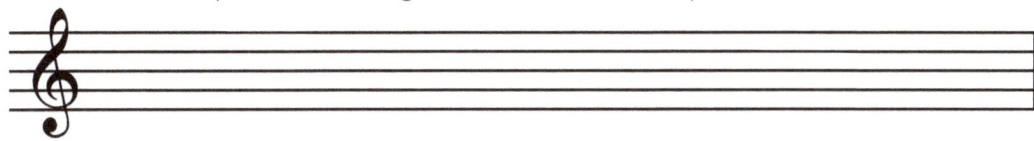

4. Write the scale of D major, descending. Mark the half steps and use a key signature.

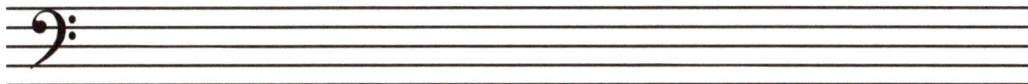

5. Rewrite this tune in the key of C major.

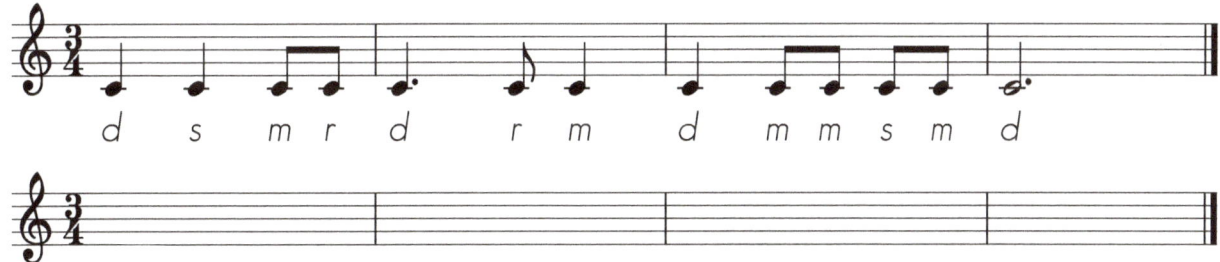

6. Fill in the meanings for each of these symbols.

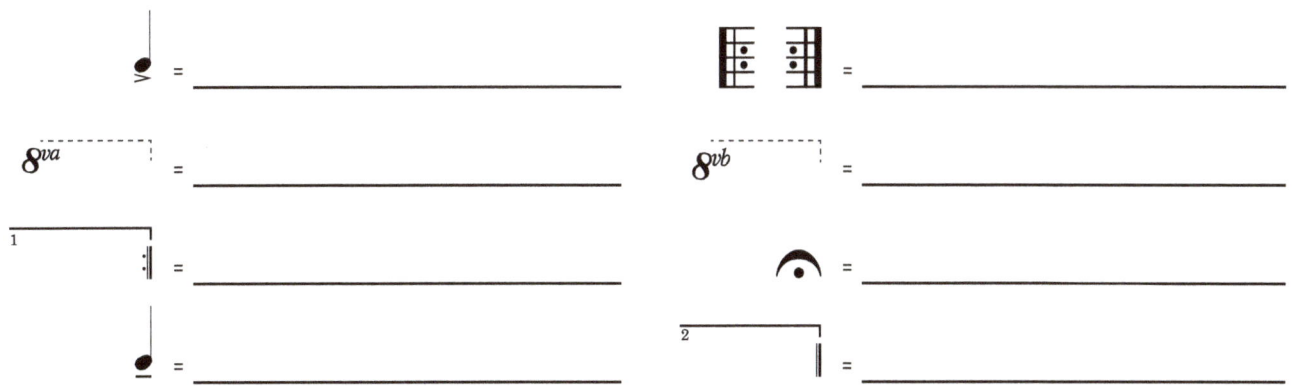

Chapter 5

Thinking Theory Book Two

- Eighth notes and sixteenth notes are beamed or joined together in groups to make reading easier.
- In $\frac{2}{4}$, $\frac{3}{4}$ & $\frac{4}{4}$ eighth notes and sixteenth notes are grouped into quarter note beats.
- A whole measure of eighth notes can be beamed in $\frac{2}{4}$ & $\frac{3}{4}$.

- A half measure of eighth notes can be beamed in $\frac{4}{4}$.

✏️ Draw circles to make quarter note beats. Then re-write each measure, beaming the notes using the guidelines above.

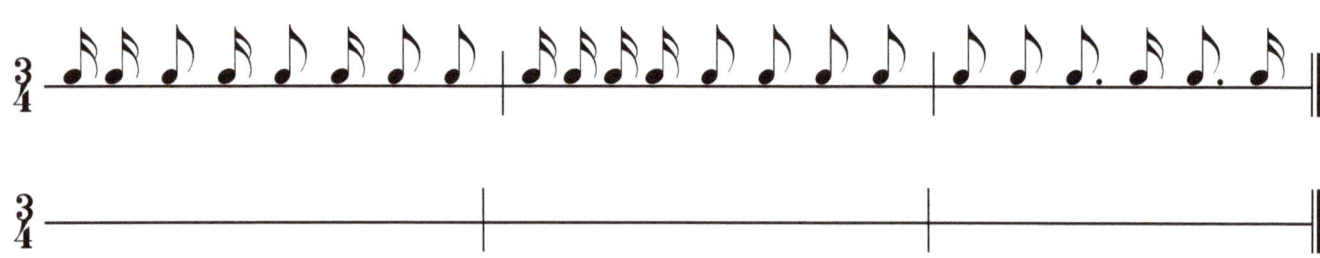

Thinking Theory Book Two — Chapter 5

> - When we group (beam) notes together, all the stems must go in the same direction.
> - If more of the stems go up, all of the stems go up.
> - If more of the stems go down, all of the stems go down.
> - If there are an equal number going up and down, the stem should go the direction of the note furthest from the center line.

✏️ Write out the scales below, following the directions carefully. Observe the time signatures & add barlines if needed. Group eighth notes & sixteenth notes with care.

D major scale, descending, in eighth notes, with accidentals. Mark the half steps.

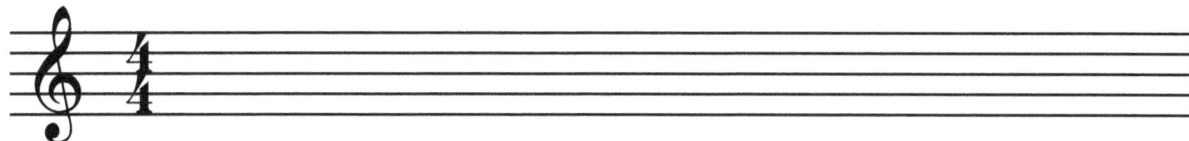

C major scale, descending, in eighth notes. Mark the half steps.

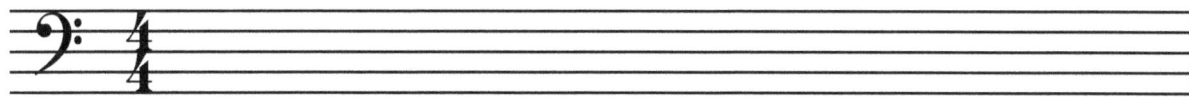

G major scale, ascending, in sixteenth notes, with key signature. Mark the half steps.

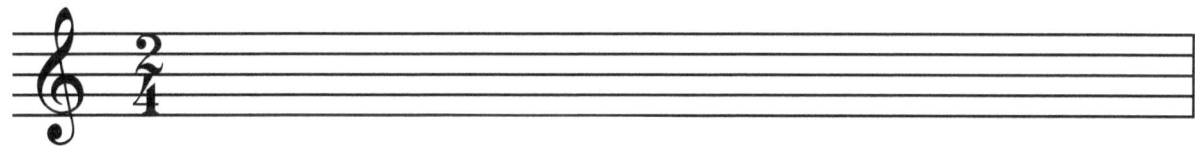

F major scale, ascending, in eighth notes, with key signature. Mark the half steps.

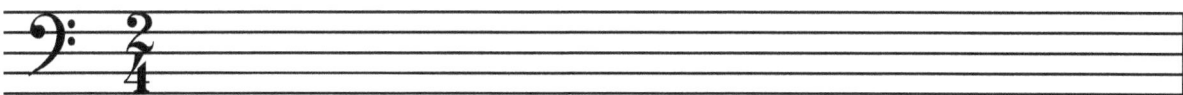

D major scale, descending, in sixteenth notes, with key signature. Mark the half steps.

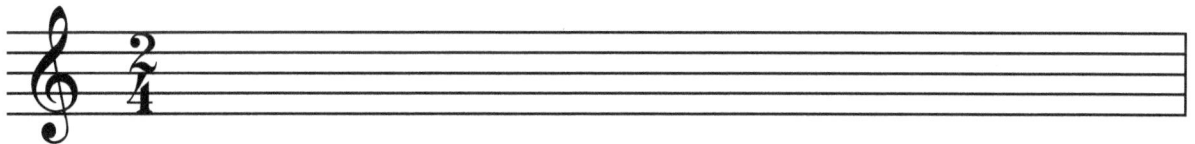

Chapter 5

➡ Rests are grouped in a similar way to sixteenth notes and eighth notes.
➡ A whole measure rest is shown with a whole rest, no matter what the time signature is.

➡ In 2/4 & 3/4 each beat needs a separate rest.

➡ In 4/4 a half rest is used for a silent half a measure.

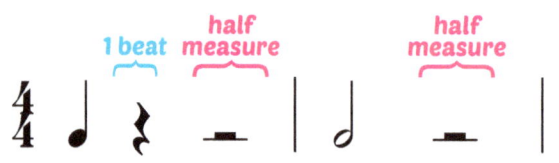

✏️ Fill in the missing rest/rests at the arrows below. Take care with grouping.

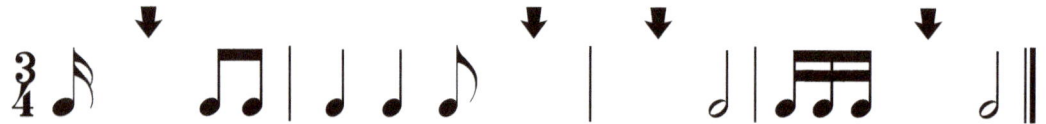

Write the name under each symbol below.

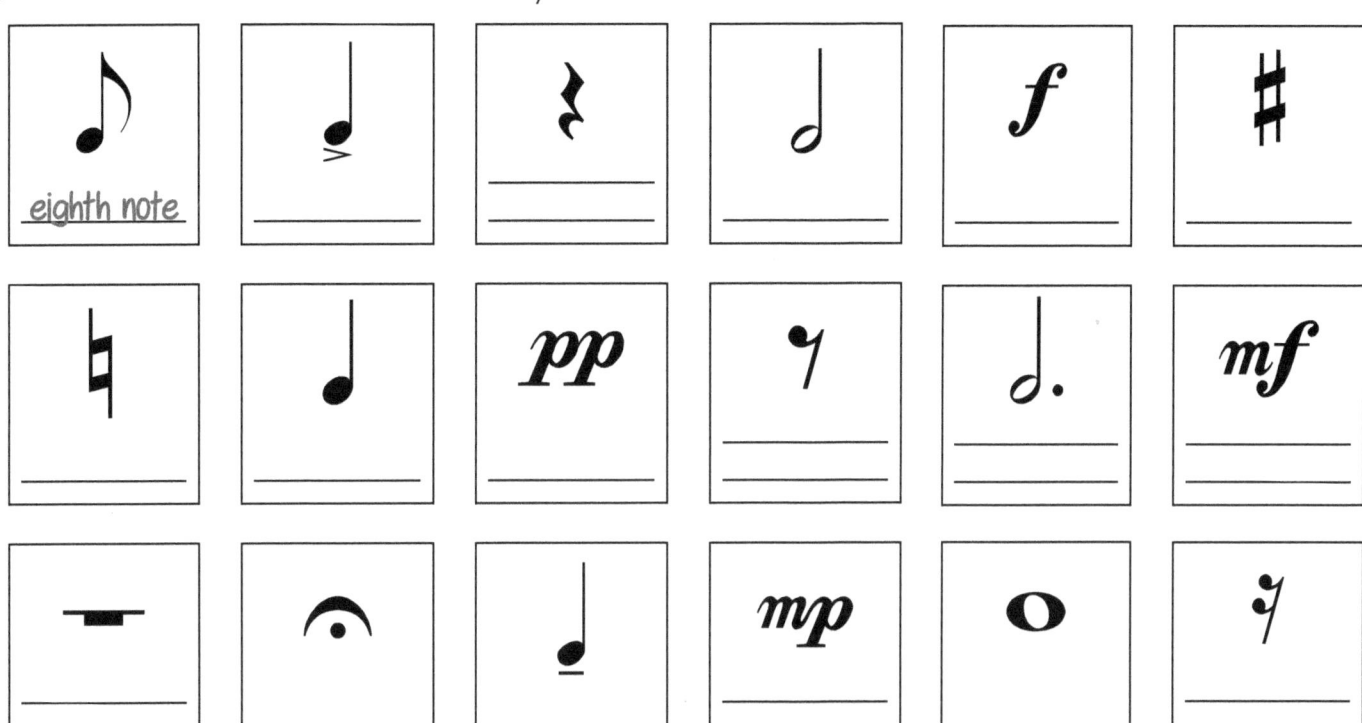

 Fill in the meaning of each word/symbol below.

cantabile = _____   dolce = _____

enharmonic = _____   half step = _____

grazioso = _____   accelerando = _____

andante = _____   whole step = _____

adagio = _____   allegretto = _____

ritardando = _____   poco rit. = _____

a tempo = _____   8va = _____

largo = _____   rallentando = _____

8vb = _____   moderato = _____

allegro = _____   poco rall. = _____

Chapter 5

✏️ Rewrite the solfa rhythm notations in each key below. Beam the sixteenth notes and eighth notes with care.

👄 Practice singing the exercises below; first with, then without, the aid of a piano.

Thinking Theory Book Two   Chapter 5

> ➡ The first note of any scale can be called the *keynote* or the *tonic*.
> ➡ A *tonic triad* is made up of three notes: the first, third and fifth note of the scale played in unison.
> ➡ In solfa these are the notes *do*, *mi* and *so*. You may know this combination of notes from playing arpeggios.

✏ Finish these triads by adding the third and fifth notes of the scales.

✏ Draw the tonic triad of each of the keys below, with key signatures.

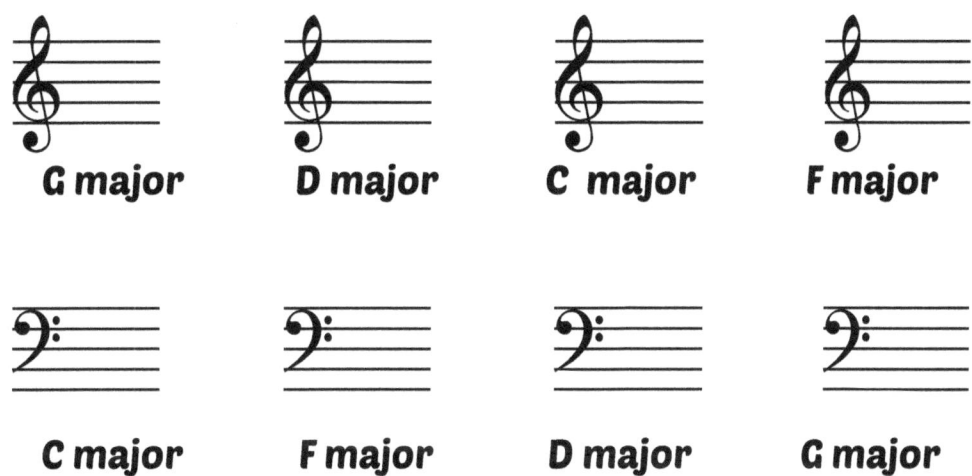

G major   D major   C major   F major

C major   F major   D major   G major

✏ Draw the tonic triad of each of the keys below, using accidentals.

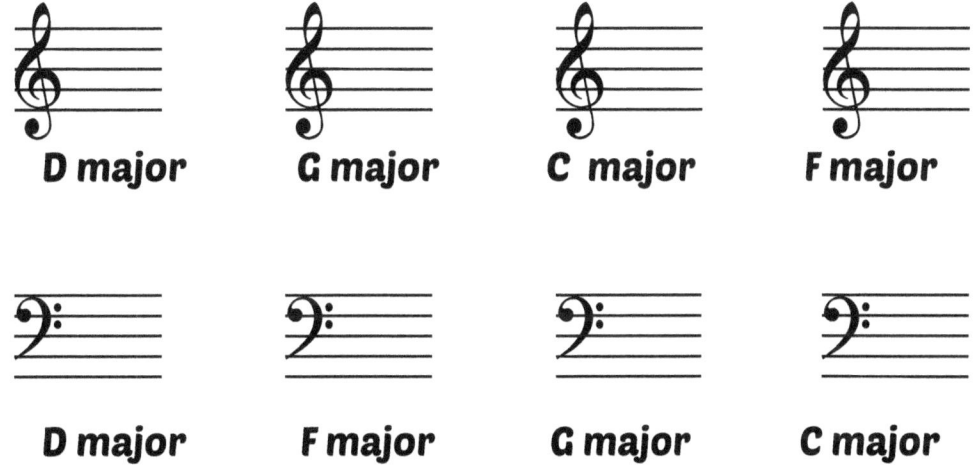

D major   G major   C major   F major

D major   F major   G major   C major

© Copyright 2016 Colourful Keys   Page 34

Chapter 5

Thinking Theory Book Two

 Draw the notes below on the staff as eighth notes or sixteenth notes.

G sharp	A	C	E flat	B

A	D flat	C sharp	B	G flat

A flat	G	E	D sharp	B flat

B flat	D	F	A sharp	G

F	A sharp	D flat	C sharp	F sharp

D sharp	C	F sharp	E	A flat

Thinking Theory Book Two   Chapter 5

Level Up!
Get ready for chapter 6 by answering these questions (without looking back through your book!)

1. Rewrite this solfa notation in D major, grouping (beaming) the eighth notes and sixteenth notes correctly. Add the key signature and time signature.

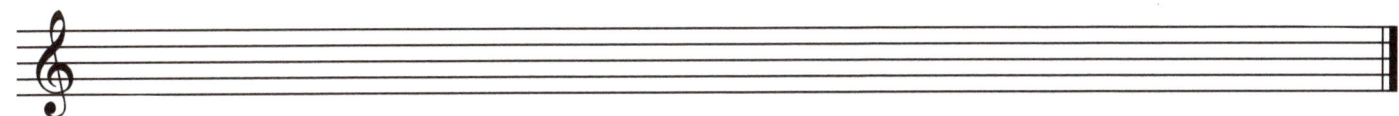

2. Fill in the missing rest or rests in this melody at each arrow.

3. Draw the tonic triad in each of the keys below.

4. Write one Italian word that means each of the following.

   getting slower = _____   quick and lively = _____

   sweetly = _____   getting softer = _____

   getting louder = _____   gracefully = _____

   slowly = _____   moderately quick = _____

   with a singing tone = _____   getting faster = _____

5. Draw the correct musical symbol in each of the boxes below.

 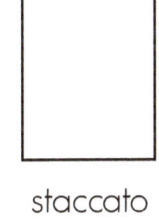  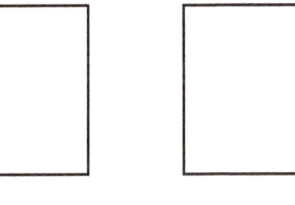 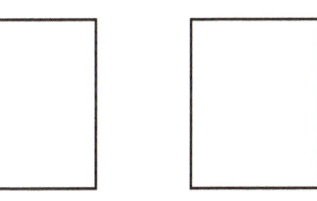 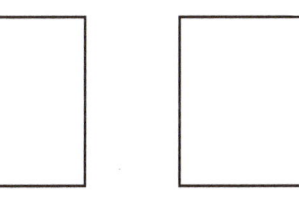

  eighth note   staccato note   fermata   natural   flat   sharp

Chapter 6   Thinking Theory Book Two

Level Up!
The final test! Answer these questions without looking back through your book!

1. Write in the note names under each of these notes.

2. Name each of these key signatures, then draw its tonic triad.

_____ major _____ major _____ major _____ major _____ major _____ major _____ major

3. Write these notes with correct grouping on the staff below.

4. Add a clef and key signature to make each of the following scales. Write the solfa names below the notes. Mark the half steps with slurs.

F major

D major

G major

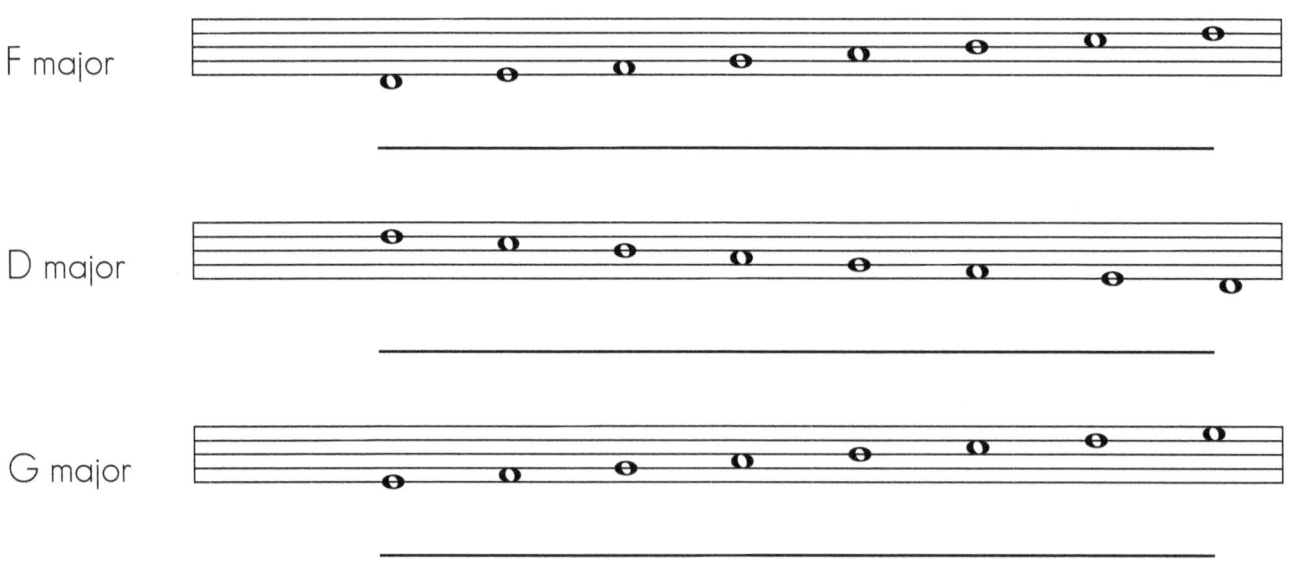

5. Describe the distance between these notes as whole steps/half steps by writing 'W' or 'H'.

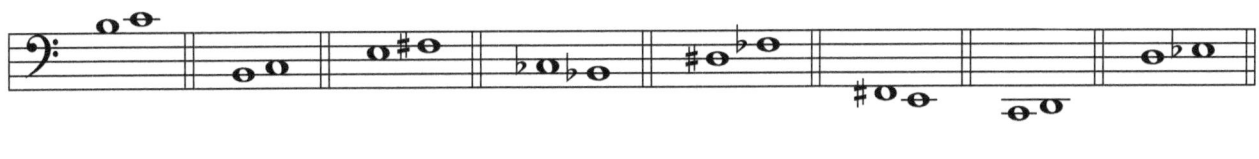

___ ___ ___ ___ ___ ___ ___

6. Add one or more rest at each arrow to complete the measures.

7. Add accidentals to put the following melody into the key of D major.

8. Draw one note equal to the value of these tied notes.

9. Add time signatures to these melodies and describe them as duple, triple or quadruple.

10. Add barlines to the following melody.

Chapter 6   Thinking Theory Book Two

Answer questions 11, 12, and 13 about this piece.

11. Add these to the piece:

    i. Write a letter at the beginning to show that the music is to be played softly.
    ii. Draw a symbol below measure 7 to show that the music is gradually getting louder.
    iii. Write something below measure 10 to show that the music is getting softer.
    iv. Draw repeat marks to show that measures 7-12 should be played twice.

12. Complete these sentences:

    i. This piece is in the key of ____ major.
    ii. The lowest note used is ____ .
    iii. The highest note used is ____ .
    iv. The lowest note is played ____ times.
    v. There are ____ beats in a measure.
    vi. The shortest note value is a _____ .

13.

    i. Name two measures that are the same: ____ & ____
    ii. Copy out measures 7-8 on the staff below. Include the time signature, clef and key signature.

Where Do We Go From Here?

→ If the student completed this book with ease, and got at least 80% of the final test, you can go straight to Thinking Theory Book Three.

→ If the student struggled with this book, and had a lot of incorrect answers on the final test, go to Thinking Theory Book Two Plus to further reinforce these concepts before moving forward to Book Three.

→ If you are unsure which of these routes to take with your student, try using some of the flashcard games with the full set of Thinking Theory Book Two Flashcards (available at www.colourfulkeys.ie/thinking-theory), to get a better understanding of where the student is at.

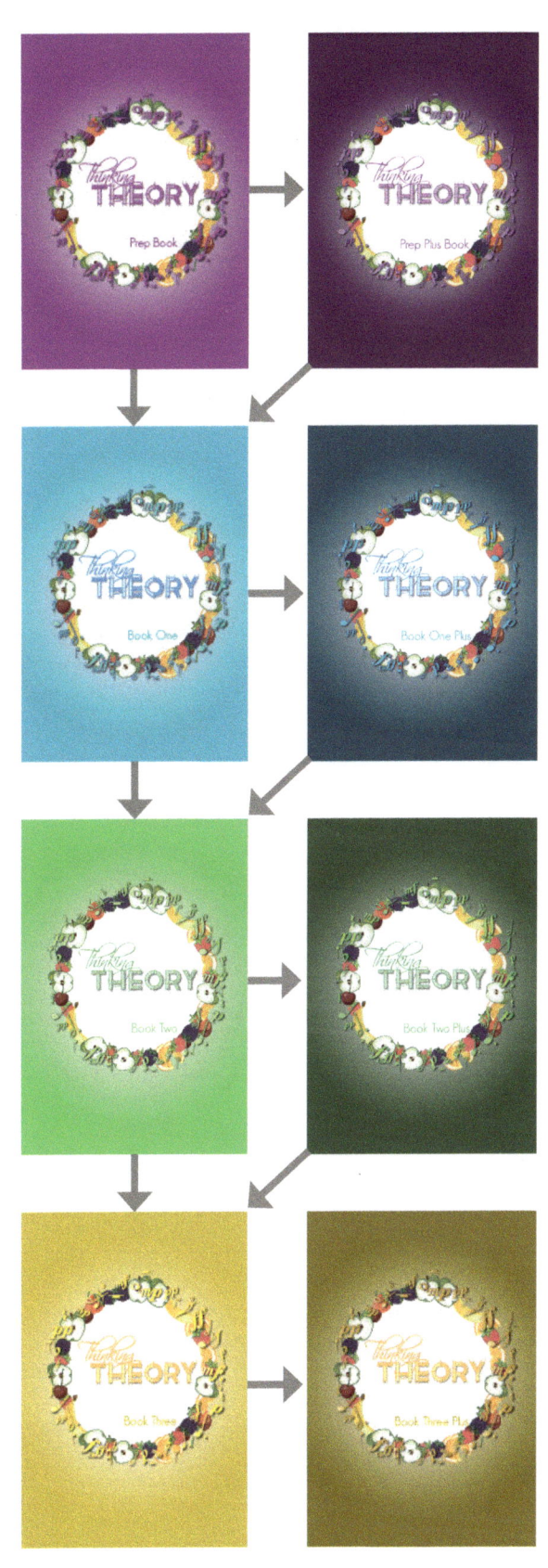

Term Review Cheat Sheet

♪	sixteenth note	¼ beat	<	crescendo	getting louder
♪	eighth note	½ beat	>	diminuendo	getting softer
♪.	dotted eighth note	¾ beat	*cresc.*	crescendo	getting louder
♩	quarter note	1 beat	*dim.*	diminuendo	getting softer
♩.	dotted quarter note	1 ½ beats	*rall.*	rallentando	getting slower
♩	half note	2 beats	*rit.*	ritardando	getting slower
♩.	dotted half note	3 beats	*ritard.*	ritardando	getting slower
o	whole note	4 beats	*poco rall.*	poco rallentando	getting a little slower
𝄾	sixteenth rest	¼ beat	*poco rit.*	poco ritardando	getting a little slower
𝄾	eighth rest	½ beat	*accelerando*		gradually getting faster
𝄾	quarter rest	1 beat	*a tempo*		back to original speed
—	half rest	2 beats	♩	staccato	sharply detached
—	whole rest	whole measure	♩	accent	with emphasis
2/4	simple duple time	2 quarter note beats in a measure	♩	tenuto	with a fuller tone
3/4	simple triple time	3 quarter note beats in a measure	𝄐	fermata	pause
4/4	simple quadruple time	4 quarter note beats in a measure	⌢	slur	play smoothly
C	simple quadruple time	4 quarter note beats in a measure	𝄆 𝄇	repeat marks	repeat this section
enharmonic		same sound written differently	8va		one octave higher than written
half step		notes directly beside each other	8vb		one octave lower than written
whole step		two half steps	1.		1st ending
♯	sharp	one half step higher	2.		2nd ending
♭	flat	one half step lower	*allegro*		quick & lively
♮	natural	not sharp or flat	*allegretto*		moderately quick
pp	pianissimo	very soft	*moderato*		moderate speed
p	piano	soft	*andante*		walking pace
mp	mezzo piano	moderately soft	*largo*		slowly
mf	mezzo forte	moderately loud	*adagio*		slowly
f	forte	loud	*dolce*		sweetly
ff	fortissimo	very loud	*grazioso*		gracefully
			cantabile		with a singing tone

Certificate of Achievement

Congratulations to

_____
(Student Name)

for successfully completing Thinking Theory Book Two

Date completed: _____   Teacher's signature: _____